Dear Carlos,

My mom is the new mayor of our town! I'm sending you pictures, and I want to tell you about her job.

Here's my mom at work. Her day at the office starts at eight o'clock.

Mom has many things to do every day. She checks her schedule each morning when she gets to work. These are some of the people she will meet with this week. Mom works hard at her job.

Mom the Mayor

by Marianne Lenihan

Scott Foresman
is an imprint of

Glenview, Illinois • Boston, Massachusetts • Chandler, Arizona
Upper Saddle River, New Jersey

ISBN 13: 978-0-328-50731-3
ISBN 10:   0-328-50731-8

9 10   V010 14 13

One of my mom's first meetings is at nine o'clock in the community center. Here is a picture of it. She says people want to decide the best way to use the community center. I think they need to have more activities there for kids!

Here's the new playground. A boy sent a letter to Mom asking for an empty lot to be turned into a place where kids can play. Mom met with community leaders. They decided that a new playground was a good idea. Mom says the boy is a good citizen because he cares about his community.

To:
The Mayor's Office,
One Main Street,
Small Town,
U.S.A.

Dear Mayor Martinez,

Here is a picture of me at school having lunch. Mom came to our school to talk about her job. She told us how a law is made. We asked a lot of questions. When I asked her a question, I remembered to call her Mayor Martinez and not Mom! She even ate lunch with my class that day.

This picture is from last year's festival. Remember how much fun we had? The people in the picture are some of the business owners who want to help organize this year's festival. I hope you can come to the festival again this year.

At four o'clock, Mom is still busy at work. Everyone says she is a good leader. I think she is an even better mom. I hope you like all the pictures. Write back soon!

Your friend,
Ramon Martinez

Now Try This

Be Mayor for a Day!

If you were the mayor of your town or city for a day, what kinds of things would you do? You might do some of the same things Mayor Martinez does. You might do different things too.

Copy this planner onto a piece of paper and plan out your day as mayor.

Today's date is _____.

This is what my schedule is today:

9 o'clock
_____

_____

11 o'clock *Talk to a first-grade class.*

_____

1 o'clock
_____

_____

3 o'clock
_____

_____

5 o'clock
_____

_____